Pebble® Plus

LET'S LOOK AT COUNTRIES

LET'S LOOK AT
NIGERIA

BY MARY MEINKING

CAPSTONE PRESS
a capstone imprint

S0-AZJ-094

Pebble Plus is published by Capstone Press,
1710 Roe Crest Drive, North Mankato, Minnesota 56003
www.mycapstone.com

Copyright © 2020 by Capstone Press, a Capstone imprint. All rights reserved.
No part of this publication may be reproduced in whole or in part, or stored in
a retrieval system, or transmitted in any form or by any means, electronic, mechanical,
photocopying, recording, or otherwise, without written permission of the publisher.

Library of Congress Cataloging-in-Publication Data

ISBN: 978-1-5435-7212-4 (library binding)
ISBN: 978-1-4747-8468-9 (paperback)
ISBN: 978-1-4747-8460-3 (eBook PDF)

Summary: Welcome to Nigeria! See the sites. Enjoy the food. Hear the language.
Discover this country's land, people, and traditions.

Editorial Credits
Jessica Server, editor; Juliette Peters, designer; Jo Miller, media researcher;
Laura Manthe, production specialist

Photo Credits
Dreamstime: Joshua Wanyama, 5; iStockphoto: Lingbeek, Cover Bottom, Cover Back, peeterv, 17;
Newscom: Africa Media Online/Andrew Esiebo, 21, Eye Ubiquitous, 15, 16, Minden Pictures/
Cyril Ruoso, 9; Science Source: Marcello Bertinetti, 7; Shutterstock: Ajibola Fasoia, 11, Bill Kret,
Cover Top, 1, 3, Brendan van Son, Cover Middle, Fanfo, 13, Globe Turner, 22 (Inset), nale, 4 (map),
Tayvay, 19, 22

All internet sites appearing in back matter were available and accurate when this book
was sent to press.

Note to Parents and Teachers

The Let's Look at Countries set supports national curriculum standards for social studies related to
people, places, and culture. This book describes and illustrates Nigeria. The images support early
readers in understanding the text. The repetition of words and phrases helps early readers learn
new words. This book also introduces early readers to subject-specific vocabulary words, which are
defined in the Glossary section. Early readers may need assistance to read some words and to use
the Table of Contents, Glossary, Read More, Internet Sites, Critical Thinking Questions, and Index
sections of the book.

Printed and bound in China.
1654

TABLE OF CONTENTS

Where Is Nigeria?

Nigeria is on the west coast of Africa. It is twice as big as the U.S. state of California. Nigeria's capital is Abuja.

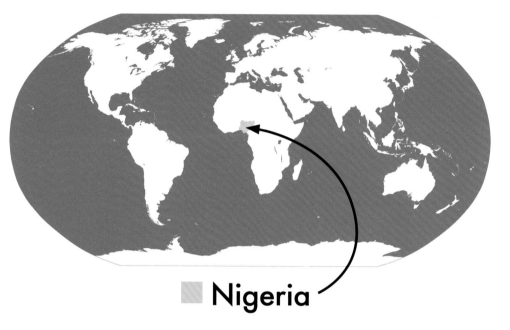

■ Nigeria

Abuja

From Savannas to Rivers

Northern Nigeria has large savannas. The south and east have mountains and rain forests. The Niger River runs through the country. It gave Nigeria its name.

In the Wild

Many of Nigeria's animals live in protected parks. Elephants and antelope live on the savanna. Drill monkeys live in Nigerian forests. Crocodiles hunt in the rivers.

drill monkeys

People

People have lived in Nigeria for more than 10,000 years. More than 250 ethnic groups now live there. The largest are the Hausa, Yoruba, and Igbo.

At the Table

Nigerians eat soups with yams or plantains. People also eat rice, beans, fruit, fish, and vegetables. In the north people eat a grain called millet. In the south they eat Banga soup.

Banga soup

Festivals

The Argungu Fishing Festival is held in the north. Fishermen use nets to catch the biggest fish. They also have canoeing, swimming, and other contests.

On the Job

Some Nigerians are farmers, fishermen, or herdsmen. In cities many work for big companies. Other people sell goods at markets.

Transportation

People in Nigerian cities travel by car, taxi, or van. Buses and trains run between cities. Many people use motorcycle taxis too.

Famous Site

Many tourists visit Nigeria's Osun Sacred Grove. The forest has prayer spots and art. Many years ago all villages had sacred groves.

NIGERIA QUICK FACTS

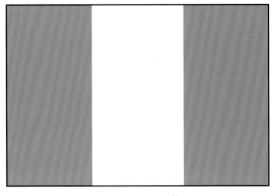

Nigeria's flag

Name: Federal Republic of Nigeria

Capital: Abuja

Other major cities: Lagos, Kano, and Ibadan

Population: 203,452,505 (July 2018 estimate)

Size: 356,669 square miles (923,768 sq km)

Language: English; hundreds of other languages spoken

Money: Nigerian naira

GLOSSARY

capital—the city in a country where the government is based

ethnic—having to do with a group of people sharing the same language, traditions, and religion

grove—a small wood, orchard, or group of trees

herdsman—a person who watches over cows, sheep, or goats

plantain—a tropical fruit that looks like a banana but cannot be eaten raw

protected—to be kept safe from harm

sacred—holy or having to do with religion

savanna—a flat, grassy area of land with few or no trees

yam—the root from a vine that grows in the tropics

READ MORE

Cantor, Rachel Anne. *Nigeria.* Countries We Come From. New York: Bearport Publishing Co., 2018.

Seavey, Lura Rogers. *Nigeria.* Enchantment of the World. New York: Scholastic Inc., 2017.

Spanier, Kristine. *Nigeria.* All Around the World. Minneapolis: Jump!, 2020.

INTERNET SITES

A to Z Kids Stuff: Nigeria.
https://www.atozkidsstuff.com/nigeria.html

Britannica Kids: Nigeria
https://kids.britannica.com/kids/article/Nigeria/345758

National Geographic Kids: Nigeria
https://kids.nationalgeographic.com/explore/countries/nigeria/#nigeria-festival.jpg

CRITICAL THINKING QUESTIONS

1. If you lived in Nigeria, what job would you like to have? Why?

2. Why do you think Nigeria is a good home for crocodiles?

3. Do you think a motorcycle taxi would be better than a car taxi? Explain your answer.

INDEX